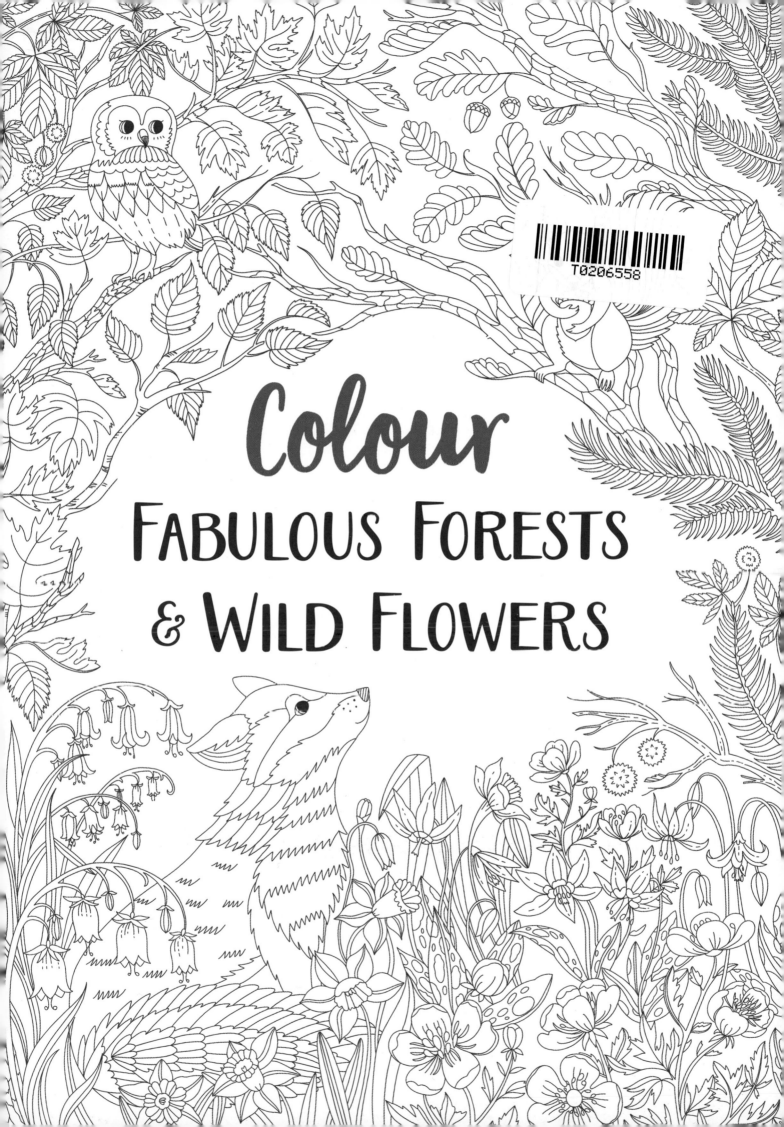

Colour
Fabulous Forests
& Wild Flowers

First published in Great Britain in 2021 by
Michael O'Mara Books Limited
9 Lion Yard
Tremadoc Road
London SW4 7NQ

A CIP catalogue record for this book is available from the British Library.

Papers used by Michael O'Mara Books Limited are natural, recyclable
products made from wood grown in sustainable forests. The manufacturing
processes conform to the environmental regulations of the country of origin.

ISBN: 978-1-78929-324-1 in paperback print format

2 3 4 5 6 7 8 9 10

Cover design by Natasha Le Coultre
Cover illustration by Pimlada Phuapradit
Illustrations by Pimlada Phuapradit, Lizzie Preston and Felicity French

Printed and bound in China

www.mombooks.com

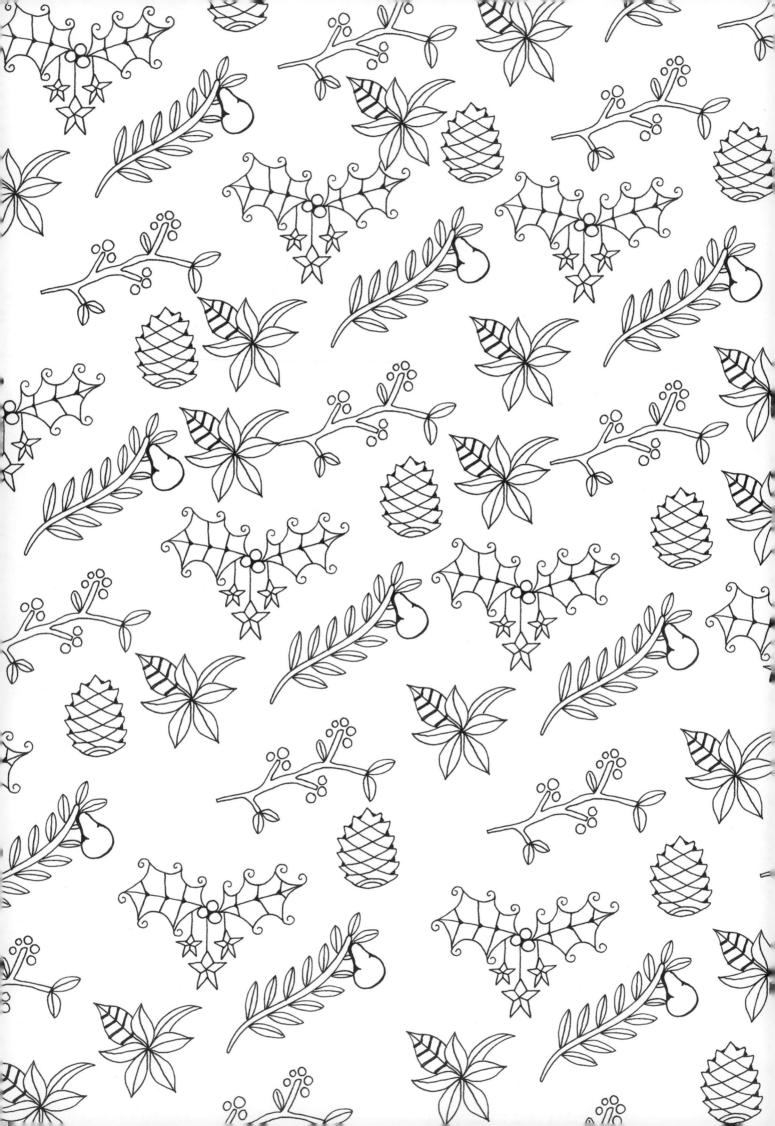